WASTE, RECYCLING AND RE-USE

Steve Parker

WAYLAND

PROTECTING OUR PLANET

 FORESTS FOR LIFE

 FUELS FOR THE FUTURE

 KEEPING THE AIR CLEAN

 KEEPING WATER CLEAN

 THE WORLD'S WILD PLACES

 WASTE, RECYCLING AND RE-USE

Produced for Wayland (Publishers) Limited by
Roger Coote Publishing
Gissing's Farm, Fressingfield
Eye, Suffolk IP21 5SH, England

Designer: Tim Mayer

First published in 1997 by
Wayland (Publishers) Limited
61 Western Road, Hove
East Sussex BN3 1JD, England

© Copyright 1997 Wayland (Publishers) Limited

Cataloguing in Publication Data
Waste, recycling and re-use. - (Protecting our planet)
    1.Refuse and refuse disposal - Juvenile literature
    2.Recycling (Waste, etc.) - Juvenile literature
    363.7'28

ISBN 0 7502 2006 6

Printed and bound by Eurografica, Italy

CONTENTS

WASTED OPPORTUNITIES

We live in a wasteful world. There are rubbish bins and bulging black plastic bags in houses, schools, offices, factories and public places. Vast areas of land are covered with waste tips. Waste gases and chemicals pour out of vehicle exhausts and industrial chimneys, into the air. Liquid wastes from factories stream out of pipes into the waters of rivers, lakes and seas. In some places, the world seems to be filling up with waste.

WASTE IN TIME AND PLACE

Is waste simply something that you do not want? Not exactly.

- You may not want those old newspapers. But the collector for the local paper recycling centre certainly does.

- You may not want those old-looking, grubby plates. But in a few years someone might recognize them as valuable antiques, clean them, and sell them.

- You may not want an old black-and-white, small-screen television. But someone in another, poorer country might be very pleased to have any kind of TV at all.

Waste varies with people, time and place.

▼ This huge mound of waste took lots of energy, raw materials and time to create. Now it is useless.

▲ The waste chemicals in these drums must be carefully disposed of, or they will cause terrible pollution.

WHAT IS WASTE?

Different countries and governments have various definitions of waste. These are usually very lengthy and complicated. Since 1994 the common European definition of waste has been 'any substance or object… which the producer or the person in possession of it discards.' But then we must explain 'discard' – 'a substance or object that has been discarded is no longer part of the normal commercial cycle or chain of utility'.

In other words, there isn't a simple definition. For the purposes of this book, we'll define waste as 'something that has been thrown away because the person who owns it doesn't want it, can't use it or can't sell it.'

TYPES OF WASTE

Wastes take many forms and types. They can be grouped by where they come from, such as domestic waste from homes, municipal waste from public areas and facilities, industrial waste from factories, and agricultural waste from farming.

Alternatively, wastes can be grouped by the main substances and materials in them. Biodegradeable or organic waste, like leftover foods and most types of paper and card, will decay and eventually return to the soil and nature. Non-biodegradeable waste, which generally comes from manufacturing and industry, is a much bigger problem. It includes glass, metal and plastic.

A DISPOSABLE WORLD

Long ago, when there were no people on Earth, there was no waste either. Nature wastes nothing, and recycles everything. Dead trees are not waste – they gradually rot back into the soil, providing nutrients for new plants to grow. Likewise, animal droppings are not waste – they rot away too, or they are consumed by hordes of maggots, worms, beetles and other excrement-eaters. These, in turn, become food for other creatures, and so on.

▲ The housefly may be a pest for humans. In the wild, its eggs hatch into maggots that eat rotting flesh – part of nature's recycling system.

A BRIEF HISTORY OF WASTE
Then came people. Some of our first wastes were piles of stone tools, bones and ashes, from the bodies of animals butchered and cooked on cave fires. Human numbers increased, and our industries and technologies advanced. People began mining ore rocks and heating them to obtain metals such as bronze, copper and iron, and firing clays to make cups, bowls and utensils. Mine spoil, spent fuels, furnace slag and burned-out ovens became concentrated, less natural waste.

When the Industrial Revolution began, in the eighteenth century, more people were able to buy more possessions and inventions, which were being churned out by more factories – producing more waste.

MORE COMFORT AND PLEASURE
At the start of the twentieth century came bigger factories, making ever more complex items such as telephones, radios, cars and washing machines. Great advances in technology and manufacturing made life safer, more comfortable and pleasurable – although only for some people, mainly those in developed, industrialized nations.

A CITY'S INS AND OUTS

'A European city with one million inhabitants requires, on average, more than 10,000 tonnes of fossils fuels, more than 300,000 tonnes of water and 2,000 tonnes of food, and it converts these into 1,500 tonnes of harmful emissions, 300,000 tonnes of waste water and 1,600 tonnes of solid waste. And this happens every day.'
Dr Klaus Topfer, former German environmental minister.

▼ Technology changes so quickly that computers, TVs and similar electronic equipment become out of date in a few years.

THE WASTE EXPLOSION

Today, there are twice as many people in the world as there were 100 years ago. Most want a comfortable lifestyle with the newest labour-saving appliances, latest fashions, convenience foods, less work and worry, and more time, leisure, money and fun. The 'old' has become even more useless and boring, thrown away for the 'new'.

The throwaway attitude is encouraged by advertising on television, and in magazines and other media, which tells us we must have the latest and newest. Giant manufacturing businesses want to make big profits, by selling more and more goods. People in less developed countries see the high standard of living in rich nations, and naturally they want the same. Because there are more people, and each person buys far more goods than ever before, there is much more waste.

▲ These paper plates and hats will be used once and thrown away, so it is important that they are recycled.

DOMESTIC WASTE

What have you put in the dustbin this week? Wrappers, last week's magazines, give-away leaflets, fruit pips and cores and bits of old food, socks with holes, maybe an old battery, even an unwanted toy or a broken gadget like a personal stereo. In an average Western household, the weight of the weekly rubbish builds up as in the graph opposite.

WHO MAKES MOST WASTE?

Householders in rich, industrial countries such as the USA, Japan, Germany and Britain produce most waste. For most types of waste, the US city-dweller is in the lead, responsible for 2–3 kilograms every day. Someone in rural South America, Africa or Asia produces much less – under 100 grams daily.

▲ In most cities, refuse collection is very costly and labour-intensive. It involves hundreds of workers and dozens of vehicles on the streets.

35

30

25

20

15

10

5

0

PAPER AND CARD PRODUCTS

ORGANICS

PLASTICS

GLASS

METALS

CLOTHING AND TEXTILES

CHEMICALS

Metals

This includes mainly aluminium drinks cans, and food cans made of steel coated with tin. There are also metals such as copper and silver in old machines and appliances, especially electrical and household gadgets with electric motors and wiring. Valuable tungsten is found in bearings, and shiny chrome and other metals are on and in the parts in toys, games, tools, batteries, metal casings, cutlery, even bedsprings.
Total: about 9 per cent.

Organics – food scraps, leftovers and garden waste

These include food waste such as vegetable peelings, garden wastes, wooden items, china and pottery.
Total: about 35 per cent.

Plastics

The list of plastic wastes is very long, from plastic bags and bottles, to food wrappings and plastic containers. There are also dozens of plastic parts and casings in appliances and gadgets.
Total: about 10 per cent by weight (but because they are light, up to 20 per cent by volume).

Glass

Glass is very useful, since we can see though it and clean its smooth surfaces thoroughly. But it is also a problem, because it is fragile and breaks easily. Glass is used for bottles, jars, beakers and cups. It is also used for light bulbs, which eventually go 'pop', and windows, which occasionally get broken.
Total: about 8 per cent.

Paper and card products

These include newspapers, magazines, comics, leaflets and posters. We also use paper for letters and greeting cards, labels and for wrapping parcels. Card and cardboard are found in all kinds packaging and packing. And of course tissues, paper towels and paper plates are meant to be disposable.
Total: about 30 per cent by weight (60 per cent by volume).

Chemicals

There are various chemicals in batteries, tablets and pills, and in discarded cleaners, paints, synthetic oils, solvents, weedkillers and medicines. Many of these have strict safety warnings on their containers. Most households do not produce a great amount of chemical waste, which is more of an industrial problem.
Total: about 3 per cent.

Clothing and textiles

Some textiles, cloths and fabrics are made from natural fibres and sources such as wool, cotton, leathers and rubber. Others are made from artificial fibres, like nylon, rayon and acrylic.
Total: about 5 per cent.

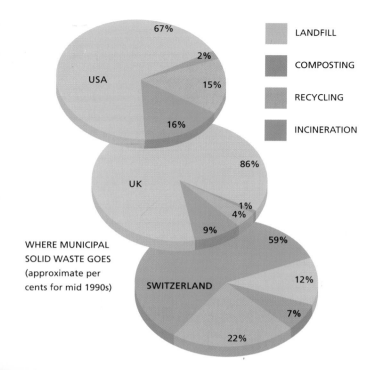

LANDFILL

COMPOSTING

RECYCLING

INCINERATION

67%
2%
USA
15%
16%

86%
UK
1%
4%
9%

59%
SWITZERLAND
12%
7%
22%

WHERE MUNICIPAL
SOLID WASTE GOES
(approximate per
cents for mid 1990s)

MUNICIPAL WASTE AND ITS DISPOSAL

Domestic waste is usually collected by refuse trucks and taken to the local waste disposal centre. Here it is joined by waste from schools, public places like parks, libraries, shopping malls and picnic areas, and some businesses such as shops, restaurants, theme parks, sports stadiums, concert halls, offices and small factories. All of this becomes municipal waste. In the USA, one day's municipal waste weighs more than 100 million tonnes. It would fill 50,000 refuse trucks.

Where does it all go? Most of it is either buried or burned. Other options, now used much less due to pollution problems, include piping waste into waterways, sea dumping and deep-disposal.

BURYING WASTE

In some countries, the bulk of municipal waste goes into landfill – it's tipped into big holes or hollows in the ground. There are more than 5,000 municipal landfill sites in the USA, and more than 60 per cent of US municipal waste goes straight into them.

▲ In a landfill site, waste is dumped, bulldozed, squashed and covered with layers of soil and more waste. The site may be capped with clay and soil, and planted with trees and flowers. But the waste is not gone – just hidden.

LANDFILL PROBLEMS

Landfill disposal creates many problems. They include smells, windblown rubbish and litter, and flies, rats and other pests which can spread disease. Chemicals, oils, solvents and toxic metals can dissolve and leak into the ground water in the soil and rocks, causing pollution. Nutrients and minerals in the wastes may also encourage unwanted blooms of algae and scum.

Organic materials like food scraps rot in the landfill, producing gases – such as methane – which burn well. They may seep thousands of metres through the ground, collect in buildings and cause explosions. Or they pass into the atmosphere, where they add greatly to the greenhouse effect and global warming.

▲ Fires at refuse dumps and landfill sites are caused by people tipping hot ashes, or by inflammable gases such as methane from rotting rubbish.

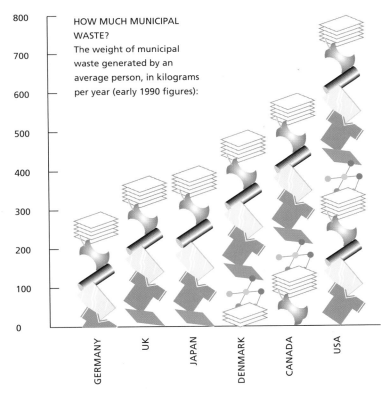

HOW MUCH MUNICIPAL WASTE?
The weight of municipal waste generated by an average person, in kilograms per year (early 1990 figures):

GERMANY • UK • JAPAN • DENMARK • CANADA • USA

BURNING WASTE

Some countries, especially those with small land areas, burn their waste in specialized furnaces called incinerators. The leftover ashes are put into landfill.

Incineration produces smoke, gases and fumes. Burning mixed wastes can produce harmful chemicals in the smoke. In some countries, laws demand that the fumes are filtered and 'scrubbed' to remove these substances. But some environmental campaigners say even the newest filters and scrubbers are not effective enough. No one knows what these hundreds of new chemicals, developed by industry and changed by incineration, may do in years to come.

COMPOSTING

Organic wastes such as paper, card, leftover foods and garden trimmings may be composted – shredded and put into holes or containers and left to decay. The resulting compost can be recycled as fertilizer. But the organic wastes must be well sorted first. Any trace of toxic substances, such as discarded batteries, can cause dangerous pollution.

INDUSTRIAL WASTE

In developed countries, household waste makes up only about one-twentieth of total waste. Most of the rest comes from industries and businesses such as manufacturing, mining, building, producing energy, agriculture and transport. So we could say that industries and businesses of all kinds are responsible for most of the waste mountain.

▲ Mines and quarries for coal, metals, and minerals such as asbestos (shown here) alter huge areas. The mined rocks contain only small amounts of the final product. The rest is waste.

WASTE AT EVERY STAGE

However 'we', the consumers, cannot blame 'them', the industries. Every day we buy manufactured items and products – a notepad or a pencil; a can of fizzy drink or a bag of crisps; a new computer or a washing machine. Every step on the way from raw material to manufacturer to consumer involves waste. We must take some of the responsibility for the waste.

TYPES OF INDUSTRIAL WASTE

Two major industrial waste-makers are agriculture and mining. Farm wastes include fertilizers and pesticides, which get into soil and water, and upset the balance of nature. As farm animals are injected or fed with chemicals such as hormones, to make them grow faster and resist disease, these chemicals get into the environment too.

To make the goods and products we consume each year, an average of 10 tonnes of rocks, stones and minerals are mined or quarried from the ground, for each person on Earth. This leads to vast open-cast mines which scar the landscape; deep mines that bring problems of subsidence and seepage; huge heaps of waste that can pollute soil and water; and ever-diminishing resources.

CHEMICAL WASTES

Industry, manufacturing, agriculture and other businesses use more than 100,000 different chemicals. The list grows by 1,000 each year – almost three every day. Yet no one knows the long-term effects of most of these new chemicals. Where will they be in 50 or 100 years?

BUSINESS FOR PROFIT

Everyone knows that cars cause problems. Making cars produces immense amounts of wastes. They produce wastes and pollution during their useful lives. And they end up as complex 'coffins of waste' containing many different substances that are hard to separate. Around the world, millions of new cars drive on to the road every year. Yet motor manufacturers spend huge sums of money persuading us to buy even more cars.

This shows a major problem in cutting industrial wastes. The main aim of big business is not to save waste and help the environment, it is to make money.

▼ Cars are complex combinations of many different materials, which are difficult to sort or recycle.

RADIOACTIVE WASTE

One of the most difficult types of waste to deal with is radioactive waste. It gives off invisible radioactivity which can harm people, animals, plants and other living things, and which will persist for thousands of years. Every day, the world's nuclear industries produce enough radioactive wastes to fill a large church. Yet there is no agreement about how or where it should be stored, or how to make it harmless.

SOURCES OF RADIOACTIVE WASTE

Most radioactive waste is from nuclear reactors in power stations generating electricity. Some comes from making nuclear weapons. Some also comes from dismantling old nuclear weapons. There are also small nuclear reactors on some ships, submarines and spacecraft. Research scientists, medical laboratories and hospitals also use tiny amounts of radioactive materials.

▼ A nuclear power station's used or spent fuel rods are very dangerous since they still contain some types of fuel. The uranium and plutonium can be removed, purified and put into new fuel rods, but this 'reprocessing' makes yet more radioactive wastes.

▲ Giant tanks for liquid radioactive waste at the major US nuclear site of Hanford, Washington, hold one million gallons each. They will need monitoring for centuries.

WHAT TO DO WITH RADIOACTIVE WASTE?

There's no way at present of making radioactive waste safe. And no general agreement on where or how it should be stored in the meantime. Some options are:

● Burying the waste permanently deep underground, in drums or other containers, in places unlikely to experience earthquakes, volcanoes, groundwater flooding or other geological events. Otherwise it might leak out and cause disastrous radioactive pollution.

● Burying the waste in the deep sea-bed. The disposal sites would be far from land and people, preferably in oceanic trenches. Over thousands of years, continental drift would gradually pull the sea floor and the waste deep into the Earth. But present international laws prevent such disposal of radioactive wastes at sea.

● Shooting the waste into space or at the Sun. This would be incredibly expensive, and there's a risk that a rocket might blow up or go off course and crash.

● Nuclear transmutation, bombarding the waste with more rays and particles, to change it into a safer form. This would use up immense amounts of research, time and energy.

LEVELS OF RADIOACTIVE WASTE

Radioactive wastes are grouped according to the amount of the radiation they give off, and how long it will last.

● **Low-level** Just above the 'safe' level agreed by most nations. The radioactivity lasts for a few decades, then fades to almost normal 'background' levels. It can be put in metal drums or other containers and buried, without great hazards.

● **Medium-level** Up to 1,000 times more radioactive than low-level wastes. It needs to be shielded by metal and concrete. Its radioactivity will last many thousands of years.

● **High-level** The waste has so much radioactive energy that it gets hot. It needs heavy and thick shielding of concrete, metals and other dense substances. Its radioactivity will last hundreds of thousands, even millions of years. World-wide, about 10,000 m^3 are produced every year. Much of this is in the USA, which already has stockpiles of 30,000 tonnes – mainly spent fuel rods from nuclear reactors.

▲ Inspectors take samples of suspect waste from a slag pile, for laboratory analysis.

TOXIC WASTE

Even in small amounts, toxic substances and wastes are known to harm nature and the environment, and damage human health. New chemicals come into use every year, and we have no idea if they will have any long-term toxic effects. Also, industrial accidents continue to happen every few years, producing a huge toll of illness and environmental pollution.

Many toxins do not break down or fade once in the environment. They spread in air and water, get into nature's food chains, and show up in animals as remote as great whales living in the open oceans, polar bears in the Arctic and seals that live in the Antarctic.

EXPORTING WASTE

'Germany has some of the world's best waste management regulations and some of the world's worst waste export laws. These two factors combine… to enable Germany to keep its home territories clean, at the expense of other regions in the world.'

Andreas Bernsdorff, of Germany's Greenpeace movement.

HEAVY METALS

Some of the best-known toxins are so-called 'heavy metals'. They are used in small batteries to power electrical gadgets. But they are very dangerous, and cause a long list of health worries when they get into living things, including human bodies.

● Lead – once used in pipes, paints and fuels such as petrol – can cause learning difficulties and brain damage. It has been phased out of some fuels, and wastes containing lead have to be specially treated in some countries. However in some places, lead is still used to make pipes, bullets and gunshot.

● Mercury was – and still is, in some places – used in the paper and pulp industries, and also in small batteries. It affects the brain and nerves, muscles, the digestive system, and many other body parts.

● Nickel and cadmium are used in NiCad batteries and for coating or plating machine parts. Cadmium is also in solders, alloys, paints and pigments and TV screens. These metals can harm the lungs and liver.

● Chromium is used for shiny chrome-plating and in bearings and hard-wearing metal parts. Yet it harms the skin and digestive system.

OTHER TOXINS

Heavy metals are only part of the toxic waste problem. There are dozens of industrial chemicals which have been found to be toxic, such as:

▲ A doctor checks a young patient for loss of balance – one of the many ill effects caused by the poisonous metal mercury.

● Dieldrin, DDT and other pesticides used in agriculture.

● Some forms of the insulating material asbestos.

● PCBs (polychlorinated biphenyls) useful in electrical goods, lubricants and printing inks.

● Dioxins made during the manufacture of solvents, preservatives, herbicides and other substances, and also released by burning plastics and other materials.

This list will almost certainly grow. In future, some of today's supposedly harmless waste chemicals will be discovered to be toxins.

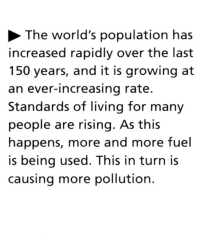

▲ Sewer systems carry all manner of liquid-based materials, from human waste and household effluent, to industrial chemicals and vast quantities of storm water.

▶ The world's population has increased rapidly over the last 150 years, and it is growing at an ever-increasing rate. Standards of living for many people are rising. As this happens, more and more fuel is being used. This in turn is causing more pollution.

World Population (Millions)

8000
7000
6000
5000
4000
3000
2000
1000

8000 BC · 1000 BC · AD 1 · 1650 · 1850 · 2025

HUMAN WASTE

The most numerous large animal on Earth is the human being. There are about 6,000 million of us. On average, each person converts a daily intake of foods and drinks into about 150–200 grams of solid wastes (faeces) and 1.5 litres of liquid wastes (urine). This adds up to an immense amount of waste – human sewage – which will continue to rise as the human population grows.

WASTED WATER

Water is used to flush and carry away most human wastes, and chemicals such as soaps, detergents, disinfectants, cleansers and bleaches from our toilets, sinks, basins, baths, showers, washing machines, dishwashers and so on. This effluent from daily activities can easily amount to 100 litres per person daily.

It may flow along pipes to the sewage treatment works, where it usually mixes with incoming waste water from industry and agriculture. Typically, solids and clear water are separated during treatment to leave sewage sludge, a cocktail of sewage and wastes from hundreds of sources, containing thousands of chemicals.

BACK TO THE LAND?

An obvious use for sewage sludge is to spread it on the land as fertilizer. But there are problems of smells and spreading waterborne diseases (see box). Also the many chemicals, especially from industrial waste water, could cause great problems of contamination and pollution.

VARIATIONS ON SEWAGE DISPOSAL

Most developed countries have laws saying that sewage and effluent must be treated before disposal. But in some places, human sewage and effluent go untreated into rivers, lakes and the sea. In areas with few people, the wastes may be recycled naturally by plants and animals. But where people crowd together, especially at tourist resorts, there is often so much sewage that it cannot be recycled. It may float about in the shallows and wash up on the beach, along with flushed-away items like nappies, toilet paper, medical pills, needles and syringes.

▼ Raw sewage pours into a bay near Rio de Janeiro, Brazil, causing a major pollution incident. There are risks of disease as well as harm to wildlife and damage to fish catches.

WAR ON WASTE

I t's obvious that we cannot go on producing huge amounts of waste. We are using up our planet's precious materials and resources, which will run out sooner rather than later; we are filling landfill sites with mountains of rubbish; and we are polluting the soil, water and air with substances from waste, some of them very toxic. We must act quickly. Some people and countries have already begun, with increasingly effective campaigns and systems to tackle the waste problem.

NO WASTE AT ALL?

Will there always be waste, no matter how hard we try? Many environmental campaigners say 'no'. They believe that by accepting that some raw materials, energy and other resources will always go to waste, we are accepting defeat. There are various catchy ideas and phrases intended to focus people's attention on the problem, including:

- **Zero Waste** We should not give in before we start. Our aim should be to leave no waste at all.
- **The Four Rs** Reduce, recycle, re-use, reprocess. We should aim to cut the amounts of waste we produce, and then recycle, re-use and reprocess any that are left over.

▲ Mixed solid waste is too difficult, costly and hazardous to sort and recycle. Sorting at source is a major step in the recycling effort.

DON'T MIX IT!

One of the major problems in dealing with wastes is that they are often so mixed up. Many different types of waste, such as tin cans, glass bottles, cardboard and vegetable peelings, end up in the same plastic bag too often. This makes them difficult to sort, re-use or recycle. Collecting different types of wastes separately, or sorting them cheaply and effectively, is a key feature in dealing with waste.

FINDING THE BALANCE

Other environmental campaigners recognize that there will always be waste. Their main aims are to minimize its production, and to find uses for any wastes that are produced.

We can all help, but big companies and governments can have the greatest effect. By changing their attitudes and using new technologies, new systems, and passing new laws and regulations, they can turn waste reduction, collection, recycling and disposal into a big, profitable and, most importantly, sustainable business.

A CHANGE IN LIFESTYLE

The war on waste involves changing our attitudes, expectations and our whole way of life. We should get used to the idea that minimizing waste is essential for our environment, our future and the whole world. This will certainly involve people in rich, industrial countries making some reductions and sacrifices in their luxurious, comfortable lifestyles.

▼ Scavenging at refuse dumps is very dangerous, with risks of cuts, injuries, disease and noxious gases. But some people are so poor that they have little choice.

BETTER WASTE DISPOSAL

▼ This fish has two cancers growing on its side. They are probably the result of industrial waste being pumped into the sea.

Waste can go in one of three directions – up (into the atmosphere after incineration), down (into landfill sites, lakes and seas) or around, (that is, recycled). The two main methods of waste disposal – landfill and incineration – were described on pages 10–11. New ideas and technologies can make these much safer and more effective, cutting the costs in terms of finance, risks to the environment and hazards to human health. Of course, they should be carried out alongside the aims of cutting waste production at source, and increasing re-use and recycling of waste.

LESS LEAKY LANDFILLS

Landfills can be improved by choosing better locations. These are checked in terms of topography (the shape of the landscape), the types of soil and rocks below ground, and the movement of rainwater at the surface and the groundwater underneath. This helps to cut down on the leakage of water and dissolved chemicals – called the 'leachate'.

A landfill can be lined with clay and/or a plastic sheet, to help keep in any water and dissolved chemicals, which drain and settle in the lowest area. The leachate is then drawn off through pipes, and stored in a nearby tank, for safe disposal.

Explosive methane build-up can be reduced by collecting the gases through pipes in the landfill. The methane can then be burned off safely – or, in a big site, burned as fuel in a power station to generate electricity. A large landfill can produce enough methane to make electricity for 10,000 homes.

◀ Instead of causing explosions or adding to the greenhouse effect, the gas methane from landfill sites can be collected by pipes, to fuel generators and make useful electricity.

THE 'WASTE POLICE'

These are usually government agents or inspectors who monitor the business of waste management and disposal. Their job is to keep a check on the people who collect and dispose of waste, and make sure they have the correct permits and licenses.

Some unscrupulous dealers advertise themselves as waste experts, charge a fee to collect specialist wastes – such as toxic chemicals from a factory – and then simply flytip or dump the chemicals in the countryside, with no proper precautions.

▲ The combined refuse plant and power station at Byker, Newcastle, England sorts rubbish, removes metals for recycling, dries and compresses the remains into RDF (refuse-derived fuel) pellets, and burns them to generate 2.5 megawatts of electricity plus heating for 1,700 homes and buildings.

IMPROVED INCINERATION

Some incinerators do not just burn waste: they use the heat that is released by burning to drive generators and produce electricity. This system could be extended to all new incinerators, and also improved further.

In a normal incinerator, only about half of the energy in the waste (given off as heat) is turned into electricity. But the remaining heat can be used to drive industrial processes or heat buildings. This puts more than 65 per cent of the energy in the waste to worthwhile use.

It's possible to get even more heat from the waste by carefully controlling the temperature at which it burns and for how long. Doing this also produces less fumes, toxic vapours and ash.

Due to problems of incineration on land, some countries used incinerator ships. The fumes were produced far out at sea, and the ash dumped there. But this has caused many pollution problems. The USA stopped ocean incineration in 1982, and it was stopped in Europe in 1994.

BE A WASTE-WATCHER

Each week the average household in a developed country gets through 4 glass bottles or jars, 13 cans, 3 plastic bottles and 5 kilograms of paper. Surveys show that nine people out of ten think that waste-watching and recycling are important. Yet six people out of ten still dump these items as waste, straight into the bin.

Waste-watching, like recycling, can begin at home. As we change our household habits and domestic attitudes, we can also spread the message into the community, schools, businesses and other organizations. The central messages are:

● Make sure any process or item is produced in the least wasteful way, creating less waste in the first place.

● Rather than throwing it away, re-use it or recycle it yourself.

● If you can't, persuade others to do so, or make sure it goes into a proper recycling scheme.

▼ Bags of pre-sorted domestic waste, as here in Germany, can be recycled quickly and effectively, saving time, money and resources.

AT THE SHOPS

We can make a great impact on reducing waste, by changing the way we shop. This makes less waste in our daily lives, and it also shows manufacturers that their low-waste products are more popular. For example:

- For any non-essential item – do you really need it? Think for a while. No purchase means no waste at all.
- Does it have to be new? Many items, like famous books or older-fashioned clothing and hats, can be bought second-hand from all kinds of sources.
- Avoid products with excessive packaging.
- Buy products for which you can get refills (for example, many washing liquids).
- Avoid disposable items, even if the non-disposable versions take a little time to clean or re-equip for re-use.
- Choose products made from recycled materials.
- Choose products made in environmentally friendly ways.
- Choose long-life products: they may cost more but in the long term usually represent better value and less waste.
- Take your old shopping bags back to the shop so that you do not need new ones, or take another bag to use.
- Buy in bulk if possible, which reduces wastes of all kinds, especially containers and packaging.
- Buy local products if possible, since they involve less waste from long-distance transport.

▶ Unlike canned, frozen or pre-prepared foods, fresh fruit and vegetables are often sold with little or no packaging.

WASTE-WATCHING AT HOME

First and foremost, sort and save as much waste as possible, for recycling. Have different bins for drinks cans, food cans, organic matter, paper, metals, plastic bottles and other recyclable items (see page 36). Also:

- Discuss waste-watching with your family and friends. Have they got any good tips you can share?
- Have a compost heap.
- Try to mend or repair things, rather than throw them away. Think of the time you spend doing this as 'earning' the money you would have to pay for a new item.
- Spend a few minutes checking that household detergents, cleaners and other chemicals are low-waste and environmentally friendly.
- Use paper where possible, rather than plastic. It can usually be recycled more easily.
- Around the house, have proper insulation, cook in bulk, turn off unnecessary lights, and use low-energy and long-life light bulbs, machines and appliances.
- Save heat, electricity and other forms of energy, as well as water. This cuts down waste during their production, and also cuts down on household bills.

IN THE COMMUNITY

Help others to realize the size of the waste problem, and do something about it, without becoming a pest or pain in the neck. Gentle methods include discussion, education and persuasion. Stronger methods include advertising, demonstrations and petitions.

- Litter is waste, and also unsightly, and a danger to wildlife. Animals get trapped in cans, bottles, plastic string and ties, or swallow bright objects, or get cut on sharp edges. Encourage people to make less litter, and to take it home for recycling.

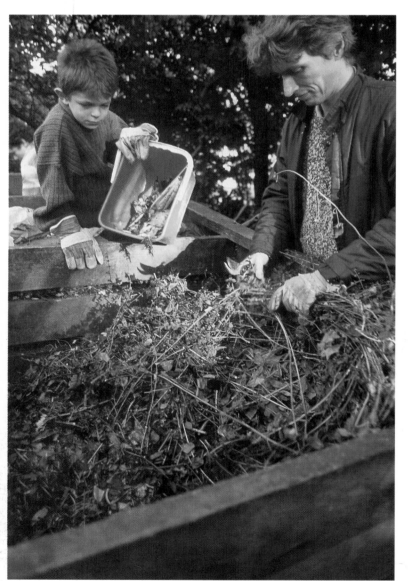

▼ A compost heap helps to recycle 'green wastes' from nature – such as grass cuttings, plant prunings, vegetable peelings and food scraps – back into the soil.

- If local litter bins are emptied too rarely, or even absent, inform the local authority.
- Report any illegal dumping or pollution promptly to the local authority.
- Ask if local schools, offices and factories have policies on saving waste and recycling. A box for waste paper, to be recycled, is a simple start.
- Write to local power stations, incinerators and industries about their waste-saving and recycling policies. Do they try to buy low-waste and recycled products? Try to get an answer.
- Join or start a waste-watch group or club.

▼ This illegal rubbish tip could hide toxic substances, such as mercury from batteries or lighting tubes.

▼ Litter and nature do not mix. Animals suffer distress, pain and injury from waste thrown away by thoughtless people.

Governments can help to combat waste by passing laws that force industries to create less of it. They can also use taxes to punish wastefulness and encourage more careful use of resources, recycling and re-use.

The 1992 'Earth Summit' in Rio de Janeiro – which was attended by the leaders of many countries from around the world – suggested shifting taxation from people and work, to resources and pollution. This means people would pay tax money to their government mainly according to how much of the world's resources and raw materials they used up, and how much waste and pollution they produced, rather than mainly on how much money they earned.

WHAT INDUSTRY CAN DO

Most of the waste in our world is produced by industries such as mining, quarrying, metal production, manufacturing, construction and intensive farming. Industries and big business have a central role to play in reducing waste. Many are already doing so.

STARTING AT THE END?

The war on industrial waste has many battlefields. One is the debate about 'end of pipe' technologies. This refers to reducing the harmful effects of waste by adding filters, screening, scrubbers and other machinery to factory outfall pipes, chimneys and rubbish bins. These remove some of the toxins and pollutants. But the extra technology costs extra money and produces its own wastes. And it does little to reduce waste creation in the first place. What's really needed are 'clean technologies', where minimal waste and maximum recycling are built in from the start, at the design stage, not added on at the end. They may be expensive to research and set up, but the long-term benefits are great savings on energy and raw materials, and increased recycling and re-use.

▶ Filter systems, such as this sludge filter for waste water, need constant monitoring and maintenance. It is far better to reduce the amount of waste at source.

● Plastics are increasing in cars, to save weight and reduce corrosion. Some plastic parts, such as bumpers, dashboards and door linings, are already recycled. Usually they are turned into more bumpers.

● About half of a new car is sheet steel in the bodywork. Nine-tenths could be recycled, provided the parts are easily separated and sorted.

● Oil filters, petrol filters and similar parts could be squeezed to release their fluid, then compressed into bricks for furnace fuel.

● Fluids such as oil, petrol, brake fluid and radiator anti-freeze could be drained off and re-used, or treated for recycling.

● Batteries enter a well-established recycling system, in nations such as the USA, where more than nine-tenths of all car batteries are disposed of carefully and recycled.

● Tyres can be recycled in several ways. In the USA, 20 per cent are made into re-treaded tyres for further use, 15 per cent are incinerated to yield heat energy, and 10 per cent are shredded and granulated for rubberized surfaces on athletics tracks, car parks and public spaces.

A FEW SIMPLE STEPS FOR INDUSTRIES

- Make parts more easily recycled by making them of one substance, not combining metals, plastics and other materials in one component.
- Standardize metals and alloys in cans and containers, so they are easier to recycle.
- Standardize bottle shapes and sizes so they can be re-used in the filling machines.
- Appoint a person responsible for reducing waste and increasing recycling.
- Introduce targets for reducing spills and leaks.
- Keep different types of wastes separate, for reprocessing and recycling.
- Accept the 'precautionary principle' that wastes must be proved safe by their maker, rather than proved harmful by other people. And accept that polluters have to pay for the clean-up.

▲ Cars and other road vehicles are a gigantic industry around the globe – and still a gigantic source of waste. Governments in the USA, Germany and other nations, and major car-makers such as General Motors, Ford, Volkswagen and BMW, are devising a scheme to make cars more recyclable. By the year 2015, some major manufacturers aim to leave only 5 per cent of a car (by weight) for landfill disposal.

Re-Use and Recycle

Waste does not have to be wasted. It can have many uses, especially if it can be recycled or re-used.

RE-USE
Re-use means using the same item again, and perhaps again and again. It may need to be repaired every so often, as with second-hand clothes and toys, but it can last a long time. Re-use has been carried out for centuries in the form of clothes, toys, cutlery, crockery and heirlooms handed down from one generation to the next. Second-hand shops and antique dealers rely on re-use. In the huge rubbish dumps of some cities, people make a living by sorting and picking through the waste, and re-using or selling what they can.

RECYCLING
Recycling mainly involves processing materials so that they can be used as raw materials for another industry. They may end up in much the same product, such as cardboard boxes recycled into yet more cardboard boxes. Or they may be very different, as when iron and steel from cans and cars are re-smelted to form scaffolding poles or reinforcing bars in concrete. The scrap metal business has a long history of recycling iron-based metals, while aluminium recycling has grown up mainly in the last 20 years.

▼ In some areas, times are set aside for people to pick through a refuse dump, and re-use and recycle what they can. But it is a hazardous process.

SORTING IT OUT

The major problem with recycling general domestic and municipal waste is that it is so mixed. A black plastic bag of rubbish could contain all manner of substances and items. These different types of waste can be sorted at modern recycling centres, but this costs time, machinery and money. Sorting at source – by putting waste into separate containers for glass, metals, paper, plastic and so on – is much more efficient.

Sorting can be done in three main ways:

- **Bring**, where people bring materials to specialized sites like bottle banks and paper skips.
- **Collect or Kerbside**, where household wastes are left ready-sorted for collection by local authorities or specialized groups.
- **Centralized**, where mixed waste is sorted at a recycling centre. For example, ferrous (iron and steel) items for scrap metal can be recovered from general waste, using a powerful magnet.

POWERED BY WASTE

Materials do not have to be recycled or re-used in a physical sense. Biodegradeable wastes such as straw, paper, animal manure and food leftovers can be composted or rotted commercially in huge 'digesters' to make gases such as methane. This can be burned for heating in homes, factories and industrial processes, or burned as fuel in power stations to generate electricity, thereby saving fossil fuels. The remaining ashes and compost are then recycled as fertilizer on the land.

▲ Clearly labelled containers make it easy to sort and save wastes in the home, and to gather them in commercial quantities by kerbside collection.

► These graphs show how Germany increased the amount of waste that it recycles. The bars indicate the percentage of each type of waste that was recycled in 1992 and in 1995.

Per cent — '92 '95 Glass | '92 '95 Aluminium | '92 '95 Steel cans | '92 '95 Paper and board | '92 '95 Plastics

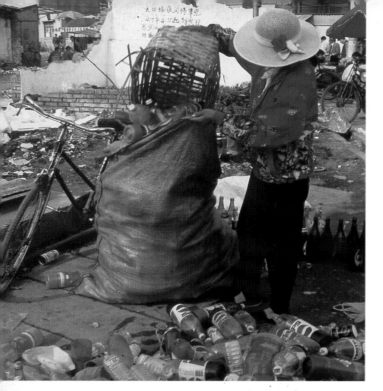

Plastics were once seen as 'villains' – pure waste, impossible to recycle. Now they can be viewed as a valuable resource for PCR (post-consumer recycling).

BENEFITS AND DRAWBACKS

Is it really worth making a special 20-km round trip in the car, just to take one glass jamjar to the nearest bottle bank? Most people would say: 'no'. The gain from recycling one jamjar would be far less than the car's use of fuel, the air pollution, general wear and tear, and many other drawbacks. This comparison of benefits and drawbacks applies to many aspects of re-use and recycling.

PARTS OF THE WHOLE

Some of the results of comparing pros and cons are surprising. For instance, compared to traditional glass bottles, many people see plastic bottles as 'bad', using up valuable raw materials in their production. But a plastic (PVC) bottle uses less than half the energy to make and transport, and consumes less than one-twentieth of the weight of raw materials of an equivalent glass bottle. It also needs only one-third as much water, and generates less than half the total waste. Changing from glass drinks bottles and other glass containers to plastic ones, can save about US$1,000 per year for an average passenger jet plane. This is because the plastic is much lighter, so the plane needs less fuel.

THE BATTLE OF THE BAGS

A scientific study looked at the resources and materials needed to make one plastic bag and one paper bag, of similar size and strength. Compared to the paper version, the plastic bag:

- Used about half as much energy in its overall manufacture.
- Caused half as much atmospheric pollution (gases and particles in the air).
- Required 100 times less water.
- Is recycled much more easily, compared to 10 years ago.

So the assumption that plastics are wasteful, while paper is not, is difficult to support. But this is only true for today. About one-thirtieth of petroleum oil is made into plastic products. One day, the oil may run out. Trees used to make paper can continue to be grown, so they should never run out.

WHERE DO WE STOP?

Such comparisons can become very complicated. For example:

● A low-energy, fluorescent long-life light bulb costs perhaps 20 times more to buy than a standard incandescent (filament) bulb.

● But, it consumes far less electricity, so over its full long-life, the total purchase and running costs are half as much as the standard bulb.

● However, the long-life bulb contains mercury, which is a costly raw material and a dangerous pollutant.

● Yet, more mercury is released in generating the extra electricity for the standard bulb, compared to the long-life one.

● And, if the long-life bulb is disposed of properly, its mercury can be recovered for re-use.

● Even so, standard bulbs are far cheaper, less complex and less wasteful to manufacture at the factory, compared to long-life ones.

So the equation continues, swinging this way and that, and never reaching the end.

▲ Long-life, low-wattage light bulbs cost more to manufacture and buy than these cheap, mass-produced versions. But they use less electricity and last longer.

RECYCLING BEGINS AT HOME

Before you throw anything in any bin, make sure that it really is waste, of no use to anyone. If it can't be re-used, can it be recycled? If the answer is 'yes', you'll need to sort it first and then take it to your nearest recyling centre or bank. Here are some ideas:

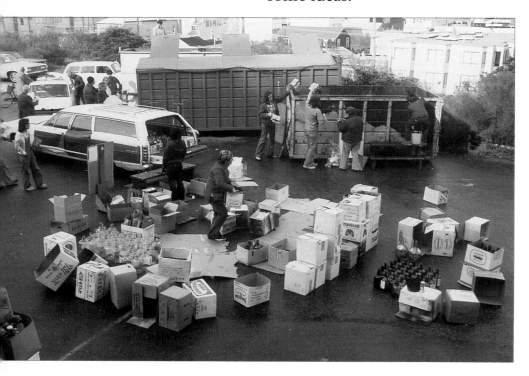

▲ A tiny amount of thought, organization and effort can lead to huge benefits for recycling. Group schemes, with neighbours and friends, or colleagues at school or work, are especially effective.

- **Paper, card and board** Put old newspapers, bits of card and card-based packaging in one pile (perhaps in an old cardboard box), and glossy magazines and other glossy paper in another. Fold or crush boxes flat, to save space. As with all recycling, check the list on the recycling bank or container, so you do not put in unsuitable items.

- **Food cans** These are usually steel (tinplate or steel plated with tin). Test them with a magnet – it attracts steel and iron-based items. Rinse them first with old washing-up water, to reduce smell, flies and general contamination. Be careful of sharp edges on lids or tab-pulls. Crush the cans underfoot or with a crusher to save space.

- **Drinks cans** These are usually aluminium. Rinse them quickly and crush them to save space. Depending on your local aluminium recycler, you could also put in kitchen foil, take-away food containers, frozen food trays and similar aluminium items.

MAKING SACRIFICES

'The real answer to environmental problems is not just recycling but leading simpler lifestyles, generating less waste, treating things with care, not being slaves to fashion, and learning to shoulder responsibility and make sacrifices.' Ken Morishita, leading Japanese eco-management consultant.

◀ Clothes and textiles from the recycling container are sorted quickly and efficiently. However, unsuitable items like oil-soaked rags can ruin an entire batch.

- **Glass** Glass bottles, jars and other containers can also be rinsed carefully, then put in the glass recycling bin. Some glass recycling banks take only one colour of glass per container.
- **Plastic** The systems and technologies for recycling plastic products are gradually improving. Plastic bags and PET-plastic fizzy-drink bottles are now collected at many recycling banks and centres, especially at supermarkets and car parks.
- **Clothes and textiles** Clothes, sheets, blankets, rags and other textiles can go into the textile bank. Check the list on the container there, so you do not put in unsuitable items. Some centres also collect shoes.
- **Organic waste** Old or waste or out-of-date foods, meal leftovers, peelings and kitchen scraps make excellent food for worms and other 'rotters' in the compost heap.

▼ Larger numbers and bigger quantities from group recycling, as here in Colombia, help to save extra time and money – and even generate income for the group.

COMMUNITY RECYCLING

In many ways, groups of people can do more than separate individuals. Numbers of people can campaign, exert pressure, raise petitions and cause change. Groups can be formed at playgroups, creches and nursery schools, in a village or street or neighbourhood, at clubs for sports or hobbies, at work, and by people of all ages – children, adults, families, and the retired.

RECYCLING GLASS

Glass makes up one of the largest groups of recycled materials. As with other types of recycling, the first stage in the process is to persuade enough people, to collect enough items to make recycling and reprocessing realistic and cost-effective. Then, the materials produced after recycling must have a market – people who want to buy them.

People in the UK use six billion glass jars and bottles yearly. About 27 per cent of household waste glass, mainly bottles and jars, gets into glass banks. There is one bank per 2,800 people. In the Netherlands, the glass recycling rate is over 65 per cent and there is one bottle bank per 1,200 inhabitants.

The recycling process is relatively simple. The glass is cleaned, crushed, heated, melted and added to varying proportions of new molten glass, and blown or pressed into new items. This recycling can happen again and again.

Recycled glass saves up to 25 per cent of the energy costs compared to making new glass. This cuts fuel use and air pollution. It also saves on raw materials, mainly silica sand, limestone and soda minerals.

▲ Recycling most substances, such as glass, relies on having plenty of material. Greater quantities mean greater savings.

▼ Cleaned and crushed glass chippings are checked for quality and colour, before being fed into the furnace and melted down for new bottles, jars and containers.

HOW TO HELP GLASS RECYCLING

● Put the correct colours of glass into the different containers at the recycling site. Mixing them causes problems and makes the process less efficient.

● If bottles are refillable or returnable, refill or return them instead of putting them in the recycling bin. They are usually thicker and stronger than non-returnable ones, with twice the weight of glass, to withstand repeated cleaning, filling and sealing. So recycling them too early wastes this extra glass.

● Expect and accept glass items which are made of recycled glass. It may not be quite so smooth and transparent.

▼ Young people are often most enthusiastic about recycling and re-use. They see that it will help to safeguard their own future.

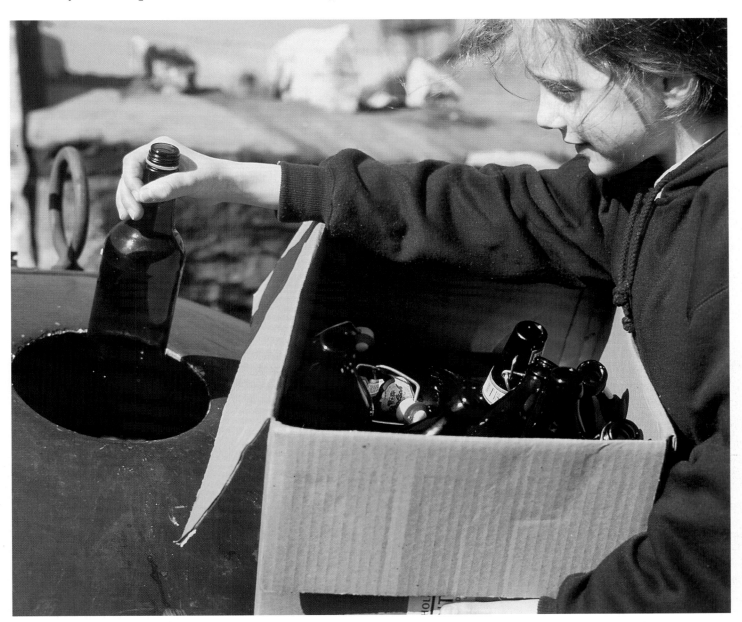

RECYCLING PAPER PRODUCTS

In theory, over 90 per cent of paper products could be recycled. But around the world, the actual figure is less than 30 per cent. Most paper, card and board products are made from the squashed, matted, dried fibres of cellulose, which came originally from wood.

In recycling, the paper and card is shredded, mixed with water and beaten by blades into a mush. This is whirled around in a big drum. Heavy bits such as staples, clips and other metal items sink to the bottom. Light inks, coatings and other chemicals float to the top. The middle section of soggy fibres is screened and filtered and becomes pulp – raw material for the paper-making process.

Paper-making consumes vast amounts of wood, chemicals, water and energy. Making recycled paper can save between one-third and two-thirds of the energy, compared to new paper. But the recycling is also a complex process. Waste-paper merchants may sort their collections into 10 or more groups, according to the type and quality of the paper.

▲ This corrugated cardboard may be heading for its fourth trip through the recycling system, having previously been high-quality writing paper, recycled notepads and newspaper.

DOES RECYCLED PAPER SAVE TREES?

Not necessarily, although it certainly reduces the number of trees we use.

● The tiny cellulose fibres gradually shorten and fray during each pass through the recycling process. So more trees are always required, to produce fresh fibres, for quality paper products.

● Paper recycling could never reach 100 per cent, as it could for aluminium. Besides the problem of fibre deterioration, some paper goes into storage, for written records and books. Also some is burned, contaminated or rotted back into the soil.

● In most countries, paper is made from softwood trees that are grown as a crop, just like growing wheat or potatoes on a farm. This is designed to be a sustainable process. It is not part of the unsustainable use of hardwoods, which is affecting the world's tropical forests.

▲ At this Danish paper mill, 100 trucks arrive daily with bales of waste paper and board. These are sorted and graded so that they can be recycled to best advantage.

HOW TO HELP PAPER RECYCLING

- Remove staples, paper clips and other non-paper items before recycling.
- Follow the instructions on the recycling container, and put in only the advised types of paper.
- Buy recycled paper products, including computer print out paper, parcel wrapping, envelopes and toilet rolls. Some types of corrugated card, for parcels and boxes, are almost 100 per cent recycled paper.
- Find out about other uses for waste paper, such as shredded mulch for compost, loft insulation, fibreboard, moulded card and animal bedding.

▲ Metal recycling is a heavy-duty process. Large sheets are cut with torches, and the heavy scrap is dumped by big cranes into powerful crushers and shredders.

RECYCLING METALS

Iron and aluminium are numbers one and two in the list of the world's most-used metals. Iron is the main metal in steel, and steel is the most-used metal in construction, engineering and vehicle manufacture. The scrap iron and steel business has been around for centuries. Aluminium production is a much newer mass industry. But purifying this metal from raw materials is so costly that aluminium recycling has quickly become established in the past 20 years.

FERROUS METALS – IRON AND STEEL

Scrap metal is sorted with machinery such as giant electro-magnets, which attract iron and other ferrous metals. Copper, brass, lead, aluminium and other non-ferrous metals are processed separately. The iron or steel is turned into a vast range of products, including dustbins, fencing, and more cans.

World-wide, more than half of all steel is made from recycled scrap. Making iron and steel from suitable scrap metal saves about 75 per cent of the energy, enormous amounts of leftover mine spoil, and huge quantities of water used to make the steel in the first place.

SOURCES OF SCRAP METAL

- Large industries which use iron and steel as raw materials, such as vehicle manufacturers, machine-makers, metalworkers, and producers of nails, screws and fittings.
- Demolition of buildings and dismantling metal equipment like construction vehicles.
- 'Junk' metal from old fridges, washing machines, bicycles, tools and other domestic objects.

ALUMINIUM

In theory, aluminium can be recycled almost 100 per cent. This saves more than 90 per cent of energy costs. It also saves tropical forest areas, which is where the main aluminium ore, bauxite, is mined.

In the USA, aluminium can recycling began in 1976. Now, over 70 per cent of cans there are recycled – one of the highest rates in the world. The Swedish rate is over 90 per cent.

▲ Mining bauxite – the main source of aluminium – means removing the entire surface covering. Even with replanting, it takes many years for the natural habitat to regenerate.

NEW CATS FROM OLD

Vehicle catalytic converters, or 'cats', were developed to remove chemically harmful substances from exhaust fumes. But they have brought a new problem of how to deal with the rare metals platinum, rhodium and palladium inside them. Instead of discarding these rare and possibly harmful metals, a new recycling business is growing up around them. The metals can be recovered and refined for re-use in cats or for other industrial uses, at a rate of 70 per cent for platinum and 90 per cent for rhodium. The USA has a well-developed network of agents who collect cats. The system is also growing in Europe.

▶ US factories produce 300 million aluminium cans daily. More than two-thirds are recycled.

RECYCLING PLASTICS

Paper, iron and glass have been recycled for many years. But plastics are a recent invention: about 50 years ago, there were hardly any. So plastic recycling technology is at an early stage.

There are many different kinds of plastics and each has to be recycled in a different way; some cannot be recycled at all. New technology for shredding and sorting the different types uses X-rays, infra-red beams, electrostatic attraction, flotation tanks and additive chemicals to identify different plastics.

WHAT DOES RECYCLED PLASTIC MAKE?

Many areas now have plastic bottle and plastic bag recycling centres. PET is the most important plastic for recycling. It's used to make more PET bottles, vehicle parts and casings on electrical machines, or spun into fibre stuffings for pillows, furniture and insulated clothes.

There are many growing uses for recycled PET and other plastics. They include bags, sacks, park benches, roofing and wall sheets, bricks, tiles, pipes, road and industrial surfaces, road cones, fencing, garden furniture, seed trays, cases for cassettes and CDs – and more recently, PCR (post consumer recycled) textiles and clothing with fleecy fibres resembling polyester or acrylic.

▼ Fence posts made from recycled plastic last longer than wood, reduce the amounts of plastic going into landfill, and are cheaper to make than metal ones.

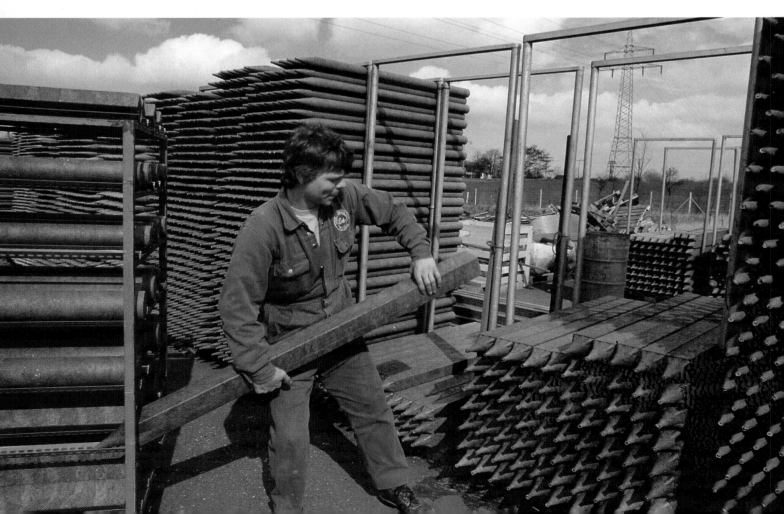

RECYCLING OFFICE, ELECTRONIC AND TECHNICAL WASTES

Televisions, videos, computers, printers, fax machines, monitor screens, photocopiers, telephones, hi-fi systems and other electronic machinery are advancing at a tremendous rate. This produces mountains of old, out-of-date 'grey goods'. What can be done with them?

- The whole device, if still working, could go to another user.
- Cartridges and containers for toners and inks can be refilled, for photocopiers and printers.

- Valuable materials in the electrical circuits – such as gold, silver and copper – can sometimes be recovered. So can plastic parts and cases, and some of the circuits.
- Basic electrical parts such as batteries and transformers may be recyclable.

Offices, schools and similar places should enquire if waste collectors and disposers have schemes to recycle electronic equipment and 'grey goods'. The more machines, the more cost-effective this is.

▶ Even though the mass production of computers only began in the 1970s, very few are designed for recycling. Instead, old computers are normally thrown away.

BIODEGRADEABLE PLASTICS

There are various kinds of plastics that naturally degrade or rot. Some are 'eaten' by bacteria, fungi and other microbes; others break down in sunlight. These plastics cannot be recycled in the usual way since they would 'contaminate' further plastic items and make them weak and fragile. Also biodegrading means that some of the resources and energy used to make the plastic are lost. After some early success, the future for biodegradeable plastics looks uncertain.

THE FUTURE

Waste has been a problem for thousands of years. Because of its ever-increasing quantities, the problem is now becoming a crisis. But there is increasing hope, too. More people are becoming aware of the need to reduce drastically our creation of waste. Waste management and disposal are governed by ever stricter regulations. Re-use and recycling are becoming big business. Manufacturers and industries are taking notice of pressure from campaign groups and the general public.

▼ Fast-developing nations also have fast-growing waste mountains.

▲ Televisions have been around for about half a century, but only now are people starting to recycle old televisions.

THE INTERNATIONAL DIMENSION

These hopeful signs are seen mainly in the rich, industrialized countries. Globally, the majority of the waste mountain will soon be produced in the fast-developing regions such as southern and Southeast Asia and South America.

THE HOPES

If the developing nations increase their consumption of important resources – such as petroleum, copper, cobalt and nickel – to those of the USA in the mid-1990s, then the supplies of all these resources will have run out by about 2020. It is easy for rich nations to point at this fact, and tell others not to increase their consumptions. But people in developing countries might well respond – why? The rich countries already have comfortable but high-waste lifestyles. Why shouldn't others? And if using up resources and producing wastes are great problems, why don't rich countries, who are responsible for much of it, stop doing it?

CHANGES AND SACRIFICES

It is impossible for everyone in the world to have the comfortable, convenient lifestyle now enjoyed by people in rich countries. It is also impossible for people in rich countries to go on enjoying this lifestyle. It is far too extravagant in terms of wasting materials, resources and energy. We cannot go on buying endless new products while throwing away old ones. We must realize that new can be bad, while old can be good.

This will involve changes and sacrifices for millions of richer people in more prosperous countries. It will probably mean slightly less comfort, choice and convenience. But it will have to happen – some time and somehow.

GLOSSARY

BIODEGRADABLE Able to degrade – decay and rot – naturally through the action of the weather and living things.

EFFLUENT Waste water and other substances from a waste pipe (outfall), which could be from a house, factory or treatment plant.

EMISSIONS Waste gases and solids discharged into the atmosphere from chimneys and vehicle exhausts.

GLOBAL WARMING The gradual warming up of the surface of the planet as a result of a change in the composition of atmospheric gases, especially an increase in the percentages of carbon dioxide from burning and methane from biodegrading.

GREENHOUSE GAS A gas that helps to trap warmth in the atmosphere and so contribute to global warming.

HEAVY METALS Certain metals such as mercury, cadmium, platinum, lead and gold, which are heavy in weight, and which are purified for specialized uses in industry. But even in tiny amounts they are poisonous to plants, animals and people, and they do not biodegrade.

INCINERATION Burning, usually at a high and controlled temperature.

METHANE A naturally occurring gas, both in the fossil-fuel gas fields found deep in the ground, and as a product of decay when living matter rots or biodegrades.

ORGANIC Part of, or a product of, or made from, a living thing.

PCR Post-consumer recycling – that is, recycling after an item has actually been used and is destined for waste – contrast with reprocessing.

PET Polyethylene terephthalate; a type of plastic from which fizzy drink bottles are often made.

PVC Polyvinylchloride; a plastic often used for blister packs, food trays and non-fizzy soft-drinks bottles.

RADIATION Energy in the form of invisible rays and particles given off by radioactive substances such as uranium.

RECYCLED MATERIAL Substances that are made by recycling from potential waste.

RECYCLING Processing items and materials that would otherwise be disposed of as waste, so they can be used again as raw materials.

REPROCESSING Recovering industrial trimmings, offcuts and scrap spare, which have not reached the stage of a consumer item. Contrast this with PCR.

RE-USE Using the same item or object over and over again, perhaps with maintenance and repairs along the way, but no large-scale changes.

SUSTAINABLE A way of using resources that does not threaten their long-term survival or the survival of the plants and animals, including humans, that depend on them.

WASTE WATER Water after it has been used by people or industry, and which must be treated (made cleaner) before it can be allowed back into rivers or the sea.

FURTHER INFORMATION

BOOKS TO READ

Work at Waste at Work by Penny Pitty (Waste Watch)

Household Waste Recycling by Richard Waite (Earthscan, 1995)

Community Recycling by Ray Georgeson (Waste Watch, 1995)

Re-use, Repair, Recycle by Jan McHarry (Gaia Books, 1993)

Clean Environment by Sara Jones (Wayland 1994)

Young Person's Guide to the Environment by John Howson (Souvenir Press, 1995)

Wasted – Counting the Costs of Global Consumption by Michael Redclift (Earthscan, 1996)

Waste Not, Want Not – Production and Dumping of Toxic waste by Robert Allen (Earthscan/WWF, 1992)

OTHER RESOURCES

A Way With Waste A video that can be bought or hired from Waste Watch.

Recycled Products Guide (Waste Watch/National Recycling Forum, updated every two years)

Aluminium can recycling packs and projects for schools, with fund-raising potential can be obtained from: Alcan Aluminium Can Recycling, PO Box 108, Latchford Locks, Warrington, Cheshire WA4 1NP (Tel: Freephone 0800 262462).

ADDRESSES TO WRITE TO

Waste Watch
Gresham House
24 Holborn Viaduct
London EC1A 2BN
Tel: 0171 248 1818
Fax: 0171 248 1404
Tel: 0171 248 0242 (Waste Watch Wasteline telephone and postal information service)
A major source of information, leaflets, educational materials and resources,

such as the Dustbin Pack suitable for 7–11 year-olds, a large range of information sheets on waste management and recycling suitable for school-age readers, and various books.

National Recycling Forum
Address as for Waste Watch (above)
Tel: 0171 248 1412
Aiming to 'Close The Loop' with 100 per cent recycling and reprocessing of manufactured items, bringing together industry, manufacturers, retailers, local and regional authorities, private and public sectors.

Independent Waste Paper Processors Association
19 High Street
Daventry
Northants NN1 4BG
Tel: 01327 703223

Steel Can Recycling Information Bureau
69 Monmouth Street
London WC2H 9DG
Tel: 0171 379 1306
Provides information about 'Save-a-Can' projects.

Aluminium Can Recycling Association
5 Gatsby Court
176 Holliday Street
Birmingham B1 1TJ
Tel: 0345 888333 (local call rate)

RECOUP – Recycling of Used Plastic (Containers) Ltd
9 Metro Centre
Welbeck Way
Shrewsbury Avenue
Woodstone
Peterborough PE1 OUH
Tel: 01733 390021

Textile Recycling Association
PO Box 124
Huntingdon
Cambs PE18 7DP
Tel: 01480 386398
Free educational booklet.

Friends of the Earth
26-28 Underwood Street
London N1 7JQ
Tel: 0171 490 1555

Greenpeace
Canonbury Villas
London N1 2PN
Tel: 0171 354 5100

E-MAIL AND WORLD WIDE WEB SITES

http://www.newscientist.com
The Planet Science pages provide topical information on many areas of science and technology, including toxins and pollution, waste disposal and recycling.

http://foe.co.uk
Information about Friends of the Earth and their environmental campaigns, especially on clean-up and waste-reducing issues.

http://www.envirolink.org/
The Envirolink page, a useful 'signpost' detailing sources of further information.

http://www.greenpeace.org
Has information about the environmental organization Greenpeace and its activities, including direct action campaigns against dumping wastes at sea, undisclosed radioactive waste sites and the hazards of toxic wastes.

http://www.diy.co.uk
Information about the way that large DIY stores such as the B&Q group are tackling waste management, better recycling and other environmental issues.

Waste Watch
Due to go on line towards end of 1997 (see telephone numbers, above).

INDEX

PICTURE ACKNOWLEDGEMENTS

Bruce Coleman Collection 40 (John Cancalosi); Forlaget Flachs 35 top (Ole Steen Hansen), 39 (Ole Steen Hansen); Impact *front cover* (Lionel Derimais); Science Photo Library *front cover background* (NASA), 6 (Astrid & Hanns-Frieder Michler), 12 (Alex Bartel), 15 (US Dept of Energy), 21 (Peter Andrews), 22 bottom (Martin Bond), 23 (Martin Bond), 27 top (Simon Fraser), 36 bottom (Hank Morgan); Still Pictures 4 (Ray Pfortner), 5 (Robert Holmgren), 7 (Pierre Gleizes), 8 bottom (Mark Edwards), 11 (Andre Maslennikov), 14 (Thomas Raupach), 17 (Jonathan Kaplan), 19 (John Maier), 20 (Mark Edwards), 24 (Peter Frischmuth), 25 (Julio Etchart), 26 (Nick Cobbing), 27 bottom (Hartmut Schwarzbach), 28 (Mark Edwards), 29 (Thomas Raupach), 31 (Ray Pfortner), 32 (Julio Etchart), 34 (Richard Choy), 35 bottom (Mark Edwards), 36 top (B Durey), 38 (Mark Edwards), 41 top (Mark Edwards), 42 (Peter Frischmuth), 43 (Hartmut Schwarzbach), 44 (Beldur Netocny), 45 (Peter Frischmuth); Tony Stone Images 8 top (Peter Cade), 10 (John Edwards), 13 (David Woodfall), 16 (Vince Streano), 30, (Jerry Alexander), 33 (Lonny Kalfus), 37 (David Woodfall), 41 bottom (Bruce Forster); Thames Water 18. Graphs and charts by Tim Mayer. Book icons on page 2, the contents page and chapter headings, by Tina Barber.